Sarah Priest lives in Surrey. She always thought there was more to life than pensions. Her love of gardening, nature, films—especially sci-fi—and tea have greatly influenced her first collection of poems.

Dedication

To the man I met the day the world was going to end.

Sarah Priest

LOVE, LIFE AND DEATH IN A TEACUP

AUSTIN MACAULEY PUBLISHERS™

LONDON • CAMBRIDGE • NEW YORK • SHARJAH

A CIP catalogue record for this title is available from the British Library.

ISBN 9781788481021 (Paperback)
ISBN 9781788481038 (Hardback)
ISBN 9781788481045 (E-Book)

www.austinmacauley.com

First Published (2018)
Austin Macauley Publishers Ltd™
25 Canada Square
Canary Wharf
London
E14 5LQ

Acknowledgements

I would like to thank Angela Brassett-Harknett, BSc (Hons) and MA (Hons), who helped me on my path to recovery and uncovered my hidden talent for writing poetry; I will be forever grateful.

Chris for encouraging me to read, especially the classics; my big sister who has always been there for me, and my dad for looking after me.

I would also like to thank the team at Austin Macauley for giving me this opportunity to publish my work and to share my new-found passion with others.

Part 1

Moments

"Hello babe," he smiled at me
As I looked into his deep brown eyes
We could have been anywhere
Chatting away like old friends
Yet, we were at the supermarket checkout isle!
He passed me my shopping; as I put it away
He had no interest in what he was doing and neither did I
I did not know his name and he did not know mine
Just sharing a few moments until we said goodbye.

Sunflower

Bright and bold, upright you stand
Like soldiers on parade so grand
Your head's held high, looking down on us all
Who knows what will befall!

Butterflies and bees are drawn to your centre
To reap the delights of your tantalizing nectar
You shine so bright with a smile on your face
You look so proud, full of grace

When summer's end is nigh, your heads droop
And it's time to say farewell to the troop
Your petals fade, wither and die
Your seeds ripen and I hear you cry

Birds come pecking to feast on your treats
You keep on giving till autumn retreats
Frost makes you crumble, you fall at my feet
And return to the earth to sleep

When spring comes around where your seeds have lain
Tiny shoots emerge to begin the cycle again.

Mother

A sorrowful sight my mother
who once was a foreboding figure
She sits on the bed like a lost child, staring into space
who knows what she is thinking.

At the moment, she remembers me, but the day may come
when she no longer does.
I see the fear in her eyes, what shall I do; she is my mother
after all, but she refuses help saying nothing is wrong, yet it
is plain to see by us all.

Her memory is fading, she is afraid; I wish she would open
up and let me in
I am here for her now as she once was for me,
the role reversed I can see
The mother becomes the child and the child a parent.

I hug her goodbye, "Take care," I say
Who knows if she will remember me, come the next day.

September

I sit and look out on my plot
Courgette plants with their mildewed leaves
Runner beans climbing still,
their tips swaying like snakes in the grass
Blackberries plump and juicy, ready to burst
Bees cling to lavender to get the last drop of nectar
A lowly butterfly flits about in the breeze
Rotten apples on the ground
full of woodlice and millipedes

Oh, how I love September,
the sun so warm and the sweet smells that linger
only this month can bring
My thoughts turn to winter as I gaze upon my
cabbages, leeks and kale
Lovely stews and soups to make
as my mouth begins to water
Now I am content as the hazy sun shines down
and I drift off to sleep...

Raindrop Reflections

Drip, drip, drop the rain
Falling from the heavens
Captured on the branches
Of inky woven cobwebs

Silhouetted by the streetlamp
The boughs glisten and gleam
As tiny droplets dangle
And illuminate the tree

The gusty wind is blowing
As the twigs shiver and shake
Eerie faces in the darkness
Make me quiver and quake

Winter isn't over
It's only just begun
Several months still to go
Before the warmth of the sun

The rain keeps falling
As I sit and stare
Thankfully, I am inside
In the comfort of my chair!

Bête Noire

Silently you come
Disguised by a purity second to none
Your uniqueness unquestionable
As you blanket the earth in just a few hours
Sins covered under a duvet of white
And now my view amorphous
You look so pretty and peaceful undisturbed,
but before too long, footprints spoil your serenity
The air is still and cold
Your lifeless colour does nothing for my soul
You are my bête noire.

Annie May

Annie May is 18 today
Hip hip hooray!
All grown up with the key to the door
It's time to go out and explore.
A holiday to Spain, your first port of call
With your friends having fun by the pool
No parents in sight to drive you 'round the bend
And tell you when the fun has to end.

Do you remember the first book we gave you?
Full of nursery rhymes, stories and fables
Your love of reading has inspired me so
From Shakespeare to the Philosopher's Stone.

So I bet you were pleased when you got
Your Saturday job at the Beckenham bookshop,
It sure beats digging your dad's allotment plot!

We had fun playing games, but for me
Your claim to fame has to be when you beat Uncle Chris at
chess
But of course he was drunk, so not at his best
So he believes it doesn't count anyway!

Your gigs to Maiden are just the start
Of a rock 'n' roll teenager at heart
With a musical soul, I hear you're heading to the Festival at
Reading
At least you're used to camping

Through the mud and rain you'll be tramping

Have fun, Annie May and congratulations on becoming 18 today!

Jasper

Jasper was a lovely dog
A black and white Collie
I had always been afraid of dogs
But Jasper helped me overcome it
He greeted me with such enthusiasm
Jumping up and down
Barking away, until I told him to calm down

Sometimes I dog-sat
And I remember this one time
I took him to his local lake
To have a run-around
He was very well behaved
And obeyed my every call
Until I reached the stream
And sternly said to Jasper, "No!"
I turned my back for just a minute
And noticed he had gone
And when I peered down the bank
There he was, having fun
Splashing about in the water
Getting a muddy coat
'Oh no,' I thought, 'what a mess!'
Jasper, 'what have you done?'

He looked up at me with a wry smile
He didn't care, he had his fun
And mucked about
While his parents weren't there

I hurried back to the car
Jasper all smelly and wet
He plonked himself on the blanket
And I didn't hear a peep
To my surprise, he'd licked himself clean,
by the time I'd got home
I was so relieved that I didn't have to hose him down
I have many memories of Jasper
who sadly passed away
But whenever I see a Border Collie,
it reminds me of that day!

My Beautiful Broad Beans

They'd survived the cold, the frost, the snow, the creatures
of the night
Nestled in their furry jackets, they could not have known
their plight.
Luscious leaves on stocky stems reaching for the sky
Patiently, I watched them grow as the days went by.

Devastation and destruction, I could not believe the scene
Aphids, had attacked my beautiful broad beans!
No warning sign was given, no defence put in place
Every orifice had been tarnished by this remorseless race.

They don't know when to stop and multiply on mass
Their only friend of the insect world, the fiendish ant.
They lure them to their abode with a sweet sticky drug
So the ants will protect them from all the other bugs.

In my heartfelt anger, I put on my gloves
Got hold of those diseased leaves and squished those nasty
bugs.
The ants fought back attacking my boots
As if a commander-in-chief had deployed his troops.

When I finally came up for air, I had a breather and sat in
my chair
I stared at my beans all sooty and black, it seemed incredibly
unfair!
I guess it taught me a lesson, if my beans look good enough
to eat

Best to cover them in fleece, otherwise the bugs will be waiting for their feast!

Rose

Her velvet touch and pinkish hue
An aroma of mystery and romance
To gaze upon a rose in bloom
Is a special kind of magic.

I've danced amongst her silky petals
In all my frills and finery
As her heady scent filled the air
'Twas a delight for all my senses.

Her love is deep and crimson red
Her sorrow, a snow-white blossom
Yet beneath her shining emerald shawl
Lies a sharp and thorny present!

She clambers up the walls and fences
Or stands tall for all to see
And when her tight buds unfurl
Her true beauty can be seen.

When autumn turns to winter
And her last petal falls
I shall keep the memories within
Until summer returns once more.

Yearning

I sit across an empty table; my heart beats, not yearning, solitude can be refreshing; no music or TV to drown out my thoughts, peaceful one might say. Yet, a loss is present, engulfs me almost. I choose to do nothing, knowing the heartache already. I can't help but wonder, to find the spark that lights from within, if just for a fleeting moment and feel the passion once more...

Pansy

Colours, so many, vibrant and bright
Cheer up a gloomy day, when the sun is out of sight

They bob in the breeze, those paper thin petals
Softer than silk where hoverflies settle

Pansies for summer, winter and spring
They top off a salad, what a wondrous thing!

Faces all painted look up to the sky
Smiling away as the clouds roll by

Sweet smelling Pansy you light up my life
Glad to have your company as the years pass by.

New Beginnings

It is a sad day for me today
Now that you are finally moving away
All the good times I've had in your Supra and TVR driving
mad
Fun evenings at the Chelsea Cruise
Watching Tottenham win or lose!

A Christmas each year full of fun
My parents loved you as a son.
Our family will never be the same
Let's hope we have not suffered in vain

Several years on, some of the heartache gone
A new life you'll have by the sea
Where you can relax in the sun and enjoy a cream tea.

That just leaves me to say farewell
On this note, I will not dwell
I shall miss you very much
Hope all goes well and good luck.

A Pot of Gold Lies Undisturbed

For every rose that blooms, a petal falls
For every star that dies, a supernova is born
For every morning sun, there appears a midnight moon
For every raindrop that falls, a river flows
For every wind that blows, clear skies will follow
For every forest burnt, new life springs forth
For every rainbow that lights the sky, a pot of gold lies
undisturbed
For every baby born, a loved one dies
For every lie told, a truth is hidden
For every heart broken, true love finds a way.

Last Tree Standing

Sad, alone amongst the concrete and glass
All my friends have gone
Once we stood together in our younger days
Outstretched fingers swaying in the breeze
Harsh winters and warm summers
We enjoyed each other's company
Sometimes, I would be overshadowed
Knocked about in the wind
But still the familiarity was a comfort
They were always there beside me

The skyline began to change
Menacing machines appeared on the outskirts
Walls began to climb
Our roots torn from the earth
Trees in the distance no more
Sadness swept over me
Disease set in, severe winters
Snow covered the ground
The weight on my branches became too much
They snapped lying dead on the floor

Spring still came and summer once more
My leaves hid the scars from the outside world
But the wound's still fresh
Autumn returned my view transformed
Piles of rubble, high-rise buildings towering over me
My days never to be the same
The last tree standing.

Undisturbed

There are things I cannot say and things I cannot do
Memories of a love affair that broke me in two
A fear of going forward, causing pain once again
Confusion surrounds me constantly
as I continue to look in.

You've seen in me the girl inside
who just wants to run away
Be free once more and have some fun
and a cuddle now and then.

Whose heart lie quietly undisturbed until you looked in
And now not knowing where to turn
except in verse and poetry again.

Secret Rendezvous

Warming my hands on a steaming mug of tea
He is late, where can he be?
A secret rendezvous in the park
Wearing red choker under my scarf
My mind is agog, my animus unknown
Watching the cars waiting to glimpse my beau
Everyone gets on with their daily lives
Not knowing my turmoil inside
To think this once childhood arena
Could be the start of an illicit liaison
Is it too late to regress?
When all I've done is had one kiss
Not that it matters now, he has arrived!

World's End

The day the world was going to end, I met you
Each minute we are apart tears me in two
I want to hold you close and never let you go
Hear your soothing voice touching my soul
Your tender kiss on my lips

I miss you more than words can say
And love you more with each passing day
You are in my heart where you will stay
Until the stars turn cold

The world did not end the day I met you, it just began...

Entity

Not a day goes by that I do not think of you
You are constant, an entity surrounding me; almost
dreamlike
One day, I will wake up; but it is real!
Some days my heart pulls me towards you but I have to stop
it, for fear it will burst
Other days it is content beating away almost purring
like a cat once it's been fed
Are you my Romeo and I your Juliet?
Amidst all this pain and suffering, will we be together in the
end?

By Your Side

Memories fading of the night we shared, making love
As the rain lashed against the window pane.

My continual drives to and from work
always thinking of you

A chance to talk whenever I can
to last the long night through.

My stomach flips and turns when we say goodbye
the last word spoken

How did I fall so hopelessly in love;
yet living two separate lives?

My heart will continue to ache
until she is by your side.

Christmas

Candles flickering
Festive tunes playing
Stockings full of presents
All I can think about is you.

Tree all lit
Gifts waiting to be opened
Memories of Christmases past
All I can think about is you.

Turkey to roast
Spuds to peel
Mincemeat soaking
All I can think about is you.

Our night together
Holding each other as the wind blew
And all I can think about is:
I was with you.

Brief Times

It's 4 o'clock and the moon is out
Yet I am driving away from you once more.

Your scent lingers as I see your beautiful green eyes staring
back at me
The warmth of your hand on my face as you gently stroke
my hair.

I am so in love but our times are so brief
Passionate kisses to last until we meet again
When that is, I do not know.

The feel of your chest under my skin
As I snuggle in tight, happy and content.

Waiting

The sun is shining
The flowers are blooming
But the petals still fade.

The trains are shunting
The bees are buzzing
And the crickets sing their merry tune.

Rows continue
Silence ensures
Impending doom

My heart is aching
Once starved of love
Will wait for you.

Love Affair

I cannot touch you, I cannot hold you
I cannot kiss you goodnight
I do not get to see your sweet smile
Or your beautiful green eyes

No holding hands across the table
Having drinks in our local café
Or talking of our love affair
And that inevitable day!

Weekends torture me
Not hearing your voice down the phone
Wondering if you are alright
Or suffering alone

I miss you every day
As time ticks by
Not knowing our future yet
Or where our next step lies

My love for you holds no bounds
You light up my very soul
I cannot imagine life without you now
As your love has made me whole.

Farewell and Forever

Our time is coming to an end
Like a dying star burning so bright
Taking its last breath before it implodes

To say farewell now seems the only thing left to do
I've tried so hard, done my best
But still it is not enough
My heart will not be the same letting you go
To face the trials of your mind alone
My nights will be lonely, they will be cold
Not feeling your body by my side
I won't see you smile
I shall miss your laugh
Your cuddles, your love

My heart is crying not wanting to let go
My tears are never-ending
I feel truly lost without you
Just come back to me one day
That is all I ask
I will be waiting
I will never let you go
Be mine forever
To start our new life remember
The one where we are together forever...

The Last Time

Will this be the last kiss
The last time I hear you laugh?
Will this be the last time I see your cheeky smile
And look into your green eyes?
Will this be the last time I stroke your chest
And hold your hand as you drive?
Will this be the last night snuggling under the duvet
When it's cold and wet outside?

All these months of heartache and pain and all those words
of love have no meaning if you walk out that door, for the
last time.

Jealous Heart

My jealous heart
Her venomous tongue
Hurting the one I love
A troubled mind
A troubled soul
Wanting to let go
A year has passed
And still you stay
Through the heartache and pain
A past still present
Trying to forget
It will ease with time, I know.

The Man That I Miss

Lost and lonely
Weary and tearful
The love I gave
Now bitter and twisted

Promises broken
Timings all out
Left in a void
Not knowing what's right

Searching my soul
For the person inside
Still scared to come out
And the truth to be told

My heart lay in tatters
My mind's gone adrift
Knowing I've hurt
The man that I miss.

Forgotten Life

What is a life, if you don't remember it?
Don't remember your first kiss, your first love
The day you got married
The children you bore, the parties you had
The meals you cooked, the cakes you made
The garden you so lovingly tendered
The house you kept so clean
The man you have lived with for 60 years
Was it all a waste?

You sleep all day, you do not care how you look
You have lost your teeth
A home you do not know, the garden is not yours
Siblings you do not recognise
And your husband, is just Eric
What a life, what a disease, Dementia!
May we never forget how lonely you must be
How confused, how much suffering you have endured
Dementia, please leave my mum to be my mum.

How Many Times

How many times have we walked these woods
spring, summer and autumn
Stomping through the leaves looking through the canopy of
trees?

How many times have we walked these hills and stood at the
viewpoint and stared?
How many times have we sat in the Lodge, me with my tea
and you with a beer
laughing and joking, remembering old times?

How many times have I driven home, only for you to slump
in your chair
Feeling alone and confused, not sure of myself, not sure
about you?

How many times do I think of you now, now that we are
living separate lives?
How many times will I keep going over the good times and
the bad?

How many times, how many weeks, months, years will it
take for me to accept what I've done?
How many times, how many times will it be before I can
finally be happy once more?

Summer

Summers past
Summers present
Summers yet to come

Summer droughts
Summers hot and humid
Then the downpour comes!

Summer hats
Summer shorts
Summer fun on the shore

Summer sea
Summer breeze
Floating in out the trees

Summer bees
Summer bugs
Chirping in the grass

Summer walks
In summer parks
Holding hands till we part

Summer songs
Summer loves
Kisses in the dark

Summer teas

Sinking feet
Pebbles on the beach

Summer haze
Drift away
Memories of those summer days.

In My Element

I enjoyed that August day,
Walking round the Sculpture Park
I was in my element,
My boyfriend was not

But we were in love
And he loves to please
So he made it his mission
To photograph me

Wooden dragons and glass-leaved trees
Dancing skeletons and colourful mosaic seats
His camera was clicking
I was lost in a fantasy

It was a perfect day,
The sun not too hot
I was in my element,
Not sure my boyfriend was

So many sculptures adorned our path
A bear and bishop sitting on the grass
Totem poles and giant stone heads
Pelicans wearing bowler hats

My imagination ran wild
Thinking what it would be like
If they all came alive!
In this artists paradise

By the end of the day
As the sun said goodnight,
My feet were weary
And I needed some respite

Some tea and cake to quench our thirst
We couldn't believe we'd taken over 400 photographs!
My boyfriend WAS in his element!
And I was in love.

The Light Is Failing

The light is failing, I do not know which way to turn
Where have I come from? Where do I go? Where am I now?
I feel nothing, not the cold, the heat, a gentle breeze,
nothing.

I feel naked, stripped of my outer skin, bare for all to see
Yet there is no one and I cannot see
I hear a noise, is there someone coming?
It's the same voice talking, shouting, crying
It scares me; the voice is so painful I want to curl into a ball
and shut it out.
It will not stop, it's getting louder, I cannot take it, I scream.

Suddenly it's quiet
A light appears, my mood begins to lift
I see a path a way out – I run and run but the path is giving
way
The light is failing; I am back in the dark
That lifeless empty place, devoid of love.

Let Me Be

Let me be the woman you fell in love with, several years ago
Let me undo the wrongs and mend the rights of my troubled
soul

Let me be free from my anxieties, depression and woes
Undo the shackles from my past to face the future, as yet
untold

Let me be free to be who I want to be, no fear holding me
back
To walk the path I have chosen and to stay on track

Let me be the one who saves you from your icy tomb
Who unlocks your heart as our passions consume

Let us walk the summer meadows, our hands entwined
Happy and content under the glorious blue sky

Let me caress and kiss your body, fill you up with love
Let's be together always, you are my soul mate, my love.

Tomorrowland

I am on the beach, holding your hand,
our feet sinking in the sand
Knowing you are with me in my Tomorrowland

We talk of getting married and when it will be,
who will come and see us
And what our first dance shall be

We make love on the sofa watching TV, laze in the sunshine
with a coke float and some tea
No demons to control us, no ghosts from our past,
to finally feel free and open up our hearts.

This is my Tomorrowland, this is where I want to be
A place that we can call our own
and you forever with me.

Emperor's Clouds and Mist

I nestle in my comfy chair to warm my frozen fingers
And cup a steaming mug of my favourite lime green
infusion

I reach for the bag and pull it out swaying as it does
Like a pendulum swinging back and forth keeping track of
time

The sweetness enriches my taste buds and I imagine where it
grows
Perhaps high upon a mountainside or hilltop in the clouds

A lowly peasant tenders the leaves and picks them in the rain
When their floral undertone is at its best and the buds are yet
unfurled

He lays them in his smoking hut and keeps a watchful eye
Until the day they are taken to the Emperor on high!

Several minutes pass me by as I ponder on this notion
To the man who brings me my Clouds and Mist, I am truly
grateful.

Love in a Teacup

Butterflies whirling
Stomach churning
First date by the sea

Walking the lanes
Out in the rain
Until we found a café

There we sat
And did we chat
As you were looking at me

Trips uptown
Clowning around
Sipping some Yunnan tea

Lunchtime meets
At our favourite retreat
Away from prying eyes

Warming, seeping, soothing
Those leaves in a bag
Recollections of the times we've had
Our love in a teacup!

Part 2

A Woman in a Tortoise Shell

I am a woman in a tortoise shell
Every move so torpid
Gone are the days I'd jump out of bed
Now I crawl out like a sloth

Every motion positioned
Like a lesson in tai chi
To ease the pain from my ligaments
And my constant back misery

I wobble from room to room
Like a 90-year-old with worn hips
Except I am still fairly young
And don't want to give in just yet!

Back at home with my parents
I no longer have a place of my own
All those rented apartments
Lining many a landlords pocket

Each year, I dreamt, I hoped
All would be fine
But now my shell has hardened
And slowed me right down

It's rather cumbersome and weighty
Although it's comforting in some way
It reminds me I once had my freedom
But now it's been taken away

My body feels worn and bruised
As I slowly ambulate everywhere
A continuous reminder of the choices made
Knowing it's too late to turn back.

Clouds

I see a goat, a man in a boat, a dragon breathing fire
It's amazing what my mind conjures when I look up to the
sky

A fun relaxing pastime when there's nothing else to do
Except lay upon the grass looking up to the blue

Visions in the clouds keep changing with the wind
One minute a wolf and a rabbit, next a fearsome pig

These pictures in the clouds tell a story of their own
Or perhaps it's God playing with my thoughts,
sat upon His throne

Heavenly balls of fluff floating high in the sky
Bring about the rain so the earth doesn't run dry

To me they are a scenic pleasure whether white or shades of
grey
With amber reds and pinkish yellows, that set the sky ablaze

The wonders of this planet never cease to astound me
I so wish I could float on a cloud and fly around freely.

Devil in a Sponge

Moist, inviting, covered in icing, the devil in a sponge.
It starts with some butter, eggs and sugar
Cream it altogether until light and fluffy
Add the flour, maybe some fruit, a pinch of spice
and voilà a tempting pud
For the finishing touches, butter icing or cream
A scattering of sprinkles and there you have it
a confectionery masterpiece.

But I must resist this devil in a sponge
It will only make me fat and I will have to go for a run,
I pass the kitchen door and there you still are
Staring at me, luring me to devour your very heart
I cannot resist, I take that indulgent bite
Savouring the moment of this sponge cake delight
I am in heaven not in hell, I know he thinks he's won
That moist, inviting, covered in icing, that devil in a sponge!

Hope

I walked in the dark shadow of light
Never wanting or complaining but knowing things weren't
right
I had fun, I laughed, I played, I cried
But still, deep down inside, I knew I had lied
Until one day, no longer could I carry on
I reached out for help, but instead fell into the arms of those
who did me wrong

I found myself out of pocket and very low
I lost my weight, my heart, my soul
Then one day, a voice inside said, 'It's alright
Seek help from those who know your plight
In the meantime, enjoy what you have, rest and recoup
Soon, you will be seen by those in the group'

A year passed and at last I got a call
They are ready to see you, I shouted, "Wahay!" I recall
Nervous and anxious I went along
I felt in my heart this is where I belong
From my very first meet, I was put at my ease
I felt calm as they listened, took notes and appeased

From then on four months to wait
Until that faithful day when Simone rang to make a date
We have a space, you can see us now
I jumped for joy, wow, wow, wow
I knew I must do this even on my own
Hence the day came when I travelled alone

Nervous and apprehensive I was still
Yet I needn't had worried as the journey was a thrill
I was greeted at the door by Angela and Simone
They sat me down and listened to me moan
Fearful, sad and depressed I had been
It felt good to at last relinquish these scenes

Through help and advice, difficult at times
I have improved and Angela has seen the signs
To my surprise homework was given
Through my collages my talent had arisen
Onwards and upwards my weight has increased
And I wait for that inevitable day when 50 kg is reached

My treatments are ongoing so this poem has yet to end
However it's comforting to write these words, like being
with an old friend.

Life Is but a Blink of an Eye

Life, is but a blink of an eye
A moment two people share
A sun-blazoned ocean
A foot print in the sand
The joy of family and friends
Celebrating Birthdays, Christmases and Weddings
Summer nights under the stars
Not a care in the world

Memories of times gone by
Keep those we have lost alive
They appear in our dreams
If only for a while
They are a part of our souls
Part of our hearts
Part of our lives
That keep us whole.

We Are Human

We create, we destroy
We nurture

We sing, we dance
We play

We teach, we listen
We procreate

We imagine, we sleep
We dream

We hope, we pray
We hate

We laugh, we cry
We love

We eat, we kill
We survive.

Love It

I love it when he calls me
sweetums, sugar fluff and tots
I love it when he holds my hand
strolling through the park
I love it when he touches my
thigh nestled on a bench
I love his ginger hair and
how it sparkles in the light
I love it when he strokes my
forehead when we lie in bed
I love it when he smiles
and laughs at my jokes
I love it that he thinks he's Peter Pan
and tells me his stories of youth
I love him in his leather jacket
blue jeans and boots
I love his fascination of movies
and all the different kinds
I love it that he's seen so many famous stars
and has several folders with all their autographs
But most of all I love it, when we are snuggled in bed
and to know he fell in love with me, the day we first met.

Monster in the Wardrobe

I'm not sure where the monster in the wardrobe came from
Perhaps watching too many Dr Who's as a child?
Maybe my parents used it as a ploy to keep me quiet
Or I had an overactive mind

But whenever I went to bed, my wardrobe had to be shut
No clothes caught in the door as that meant he could break
out
He was scared of the landing light, so that was left on at
night

My feet and hands tucked away in case this should entice
the monster from his lair
Quiet and unobtrusive, no one would know he was there
Yet when night time came and I was ready to sleep
He was always lurking, hiding, in the wardrobe at the end of
my bed.

Pensions

Pensions, pensions, please someone give me a sign when I
should draw my pension
Do I take it early at 55 or wait until I am 75?
My funds are on a rollercoaster going up and down
Playing FTSE in the market place,
they never touch the ground
Do I leave it in a managed fund or risk it in Japan
Take a drawdown policy and get my 25% tax free
Or cash it all in and buy myself a Ferrari
If I am overweight or had a stroke, my luck might be in
I can get an impaired annuity so cakes are no longer a sin!

I could invest in a low-risk fund but there's no guarantee
Every insurance company tells me, I might not get back
what I put in!
Maybe I should keep working and top-up my pot
Who knows the stock market might boom and it will be like
winning the jackpot
Yet I know only too well the crashes from the past
Black Monday, Black Friday thank heavens it didn't last
I'm beginning to think that pensions is just pot luck
So I don't think I'll worry, cos the day I draw my pension I
might get run over by a bus!

Sick Water Tank

There is a sick water tank in the kitchen at work
It has a plaster on its nose
How thoughtful someone must have been
Who saw the dripping water flow
To put a bandage on its nose

Alas, the plaster was not enough
To stop the dripping water flow
So now the kitchen floor is wet
And the water tank has lost its nose!

Skyped Love

Dinner for one sat by a screen
So I can see my loved one,
I can talk with him, laugh with him
While away the hours, both stuck in our cells
Him on his bed feeling rather depressed

But this is not how it was meant to be
We tried to buy a home
Got stymied from every direction
I became ill, my back ceased
So we both ended up at our parents'

I try to imagine if we'd met long ago
Before the invention of automobiles and telephones
Our only communication sending
love letters in the post
Would my yen be any less?
Would my pain be any worse?

So even in this technological age
I get a glimpse of him everyday
But still it hasn't helped
Buy a house, ease my conscience or my pain

All it does is remind me
each and every day
I am still not with him
as he is living far away.

Somewhere

When I desert this earthly coil
I know I'll still be on the boil – somewhere

When earthly senses have me seem
A fading memory, a cloud of steam
I'll chuckle with my eyes agleam – somewhere

When time decrees by nature's rote
I don again a mortal coat
I'll yell and rock the earthly boat – somewhere

And know for sure that there will be
A time I meet you and you meet me
We'll chat again o'er Lapsang tea – somewhere.

– My neighbour

The Love Witch

My boyfriend thinks I'm a love witch
I've put a spell on him
He fell in love with me instantly
The day we first met

He thinks I have some effigy
And potions at home
A secret altar where one day
I'll sacrifice him like the Wicker Man

I am not sure why he has this impression
I don't look much like a witch
I don't own a cauldron, black cat or broomstick!

He's never been in love before
So maybe that's why
His head is in constant turmoil
And his emotions have run wild

The chemical reaction
When you first fall in love
Wanting to be with your lover
No matter what the cost

It is kinda fun and
I might keep up the pretence
That I am this love witch
And I've put a spell on him!

Tomato in a Cake Tin

I knew something was up, old age, just a little forgetful
Or was it something more sinister like Dementia!
I found a tomato in a cake tin, oh we did laugh
Milk in the cupboard, searching for her specs
Then she became vacant sitting on her bed
Of course it got worse, Mum in denial
She lost interest in cooking and even the house
She calls out at night for her sister Jean
Her clothes are all sticky, I call her the marmalade queen
Occasionally we'd chat, I told her she was married,
"How long has it been?" "60 years," I added
"Oh dear," she replied, "best find myself a new fella."

She's still in there somewhere with her odd little ways
When I am watching a movie she'd often say
"I've seen that already"
But I know she's mistaken as it's never been on the telly
She ate all my sweet potatoes one day
I'd left them in the kitchen, cooling on a tray
"Did you eat them?" I asked. "Of course not," she snapped,
"I don't even like them!"
She plays this shushing game with my beau, I think she
doesn't want to be seen
She calls him stupid, sometimes handsome but she doesn't
know who he is
I know it's downhill from now on and I will miss her when
she is gone
But I will always remember the tomato in the cake tin and
how it made us all laugh back then.

Sanctuary

I bought myself a cushion
With a picture of a shed
It reminds me of my allotment
Where now I hardly tread

I remember the day I went there
In the hope of renting a plot
It was a cold January morning
I was wrapped in my raincoat, boots and gloves

After seeing only a few
It was the last one on the list
I immediately fell in love
'Cos it had its own shed!

Ten years have now passed
Many a weekend spent
Tending the earth, digging beds
Pruning, weeding, enjoying the freedom
Growing my own veg

I made a garden full of flowers
Sometimes it got a little wild
I loved watching the bees
In my digitalis
Butterflies dancing the zephyr
And crickets jumping all around

I seldom visit my sanctuary

As that is what it was
The break-up of a relationship
Helped the demise of my plot

No more sowing seeds,
Reading all those gardening magazines
Chatting with old friends
Enjoying a place where I could be me

I am rather broken to know it's gone
It replenished my soul, gave me a purpose
It was a place I called home.

The Second-Hand Bookshop

The second-hand bookshop meant nothing in my youth
For I had no passion for reading
But now to stumble upon such stores
Is like stepping into a cave full of historical gems
Shelves upon shelves laden with treasures
When I open a book, I'm travelling through time
Going back to bygone days living in a past
Where different words had different meanings
Some no longer uttered
Some their meanings have changed

Dirty worn pages all yellowy brown
Many people have fingered these leaves
The author now passed but when I read
They instantly come alive
Their words tantalize my mind
Enlighten my soul
Have the power to change my destiny

The covers are works of art
The quirkiness, the silence, quieter than a library
The bookworms that enter this realm of words
An experience you'd never get searching the net

Two volumes of war and peace on the counter
The complete works of the Bible
Nearly as big as my torso
I'd have to live a thousand years to read it!
I could stay here for hours, but the clock's ticking

As I make my way from the attic
My arms laden with books as I hand them to the seller
Who beams at me, "My you've got one from every section."
My excitement within for the joys these books bring
Having taken away a few gems from his store.

Death in a Teacup

All alone at the café
Cup of tea for one
The decor has changed, the seating all worn
The arcade game we played now gone

No butterflies churning
Looking into your puppy-dog eyes
Holding your hand across the table
Those long kisses goodbye

I take a sip of my lukewarm tea
Doesn't taste like it once did
Acerbic and unpleasant,
I shudder as it passes my lips

I stare at the rings of life
Clasping this cup in my hands
Once it felt warm and inviting
Now it tells a different tale

I watch the comings and goings of the people
Heads down on their mobiles and tablets
The modern life we live in
Oblivious to what's going on around them

It all began here at the Lansdowne
Where we'd meet for a cuppa and some food
We'd chat away for hours
As our love grew and grew

Now those times have gone
And I am alone with my tea for one
The murky green dregs at the bottom
Fill me with sadness, my death in a tea cup.

What Is Love?

Is it passion, control, contentment, happiness or freedom?
Is it belonging, companionship a need to be needed?
Is it desire, an obsession, stifling or all-consuming?
Is it in the mind or does it come from the heart?

Does it make you crazy, angry or upset?
Does it make you strong, confident or weak?
Does it make you frustrated?
Want to cry, want to die?

It does make you do things
you never would have dreamed
It does control your mind, your heart,
it does make you believe.

It is a powerful force that can enrich your life
and one that can destroy your very soul.
It is love, that enigma in life,
It is love, love, love.

For All the Days

For all the days the sun has shone
And all the days the rain has come
For all the times I've gazed at the stars
And seen the face of the moon.

For all the steps I have walked
In a field, by the roadside, in my home
For all the words I have spoken
To the many I have met.

For all the unspoken words
That keep me awake at night
And wish that I had said.

For all the seeds I have planted
Watered, nurtured, watched them grow
Watched them wither and some I have eaten.

For all the films I have seen
Too many to mention
And for all those still to come
I wait in anticipation.

For all the poems I have read
That touch my heart
The sadness, the joy
The human part of life.

For all the days that are gone

And for all the days yet to come
I wish I could have understood
The world my mother lived in.

Forever Lost

I wish for life
In a vacant face
Does she know me
Deep down inside
Or am I erased
From her mind
Like I was never born?

A one-sided story
More fiction than fact
I cannot reminisce
Laugh at the good old days
Watching her daily
Wanting to escape
To a world only she knows.

I wish I could take her there
To see a familiar face
A familiar place
And watch her smile
To imagine where she is
Fills me with dread
There's no escape
Forever lost
In the maze of her mind.

I've Lost My Mum to Dementia

I've lost my mum to Dementia
Three years and counting
Living with her constantly
Watching her struggle.

I miss her treacle puddings
Apple pies and sponges
I miss our chats
Her over-anxious mind.

I miss the family gatherings
When we had Uncle Leon for tea
We'd sit in the garden
Till the sun had gone behind the trees.

I miss her artistic flair
The cakes and flowers she made
I miss all the Christmas fayre
And the table nicely laid.

I miss her more than ever
As the weeks roll into one
She has no life, she's lost her mind
I cry inside at night.

Knowing she has gone
Knowing she will never come back

What a horrible and cruel way
To live the last years of one's life.